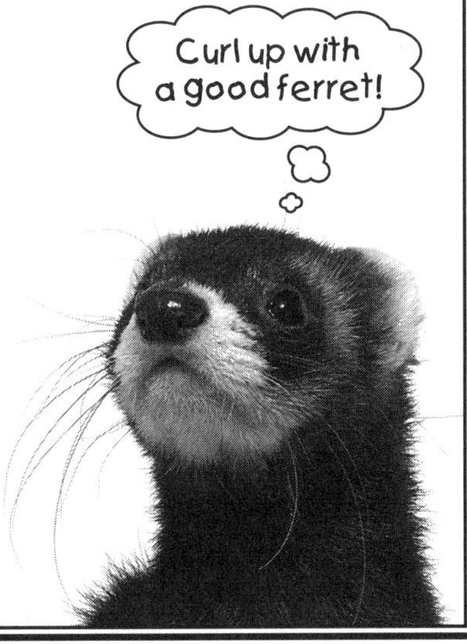
Curl up with
a good ferret!

Introduction

Who can resist the charm of a ferret? I certainly can't. I'll bet you're the same as I am: you see that little pink (or brown or dappled) nose, the white-rimmed ears, or the joyful little dance, and you're hooked.

Of course, ferrets aren't all fun and games (for us, I mean). Sometimes the little rascals can make us crazier than we already are! But that's part of why we love them so much.

Wouldn't it be wonderful if we knew what our ferrets are thinking? You know you want to know. So curl up with a nice warm ferret (if you can get him or her to sit still) and read on. I'm sure you'll be delighted.

— Mary R. Shefferman

500 Things My Ferret Told Me

Curl up with a good ferret!

You'll laugh. You'll learn. You'll love your ferret!

Copyright ©2002 Mary R. Shefferman. All rights reserved.
No part of this book may be used or reproduced in any manner
whatsoever without the prior written permission of the publisher,
except in the case of brief quotations embodied in critical articles
and reviews.

A "500 Things" book produced under license from Adam Post.
Manufactured in the United States of America
Library of Congress Control Number: 2002108986
ISBN 0-9667073-2-X

Publisher's Cataloging-in-Publication Data
Shefferman, Mary R.
    500 Things My Ferret Told Me:
    You'll laugh. You'll learn. You'll love your ferret.
        p.   cm.
    ISBN 0-9667073-2-X
    1. Ferrets as pets 2. Happiness—Quotations, maxims,
    etc. 3. Conduct of life—Quotations, maxims, etc.
    I. Shefferman, Mary R. 1963-
  II. Title
  SF459.F47   2002
  636.976628-dc20   2002108986

Modern Ferret • PO Box 1007 • Smithtown NY 11787
www.modernferret.com • www.ferrettradingpost.com

Dedicated to the Modern Ferrets *who inspired it all:*

Sabrina
Ralph
Marshmallow
Knuks
Trixie
Bosco da Gama
Balthazar
Cauliflower
Koosh
Gabrielle

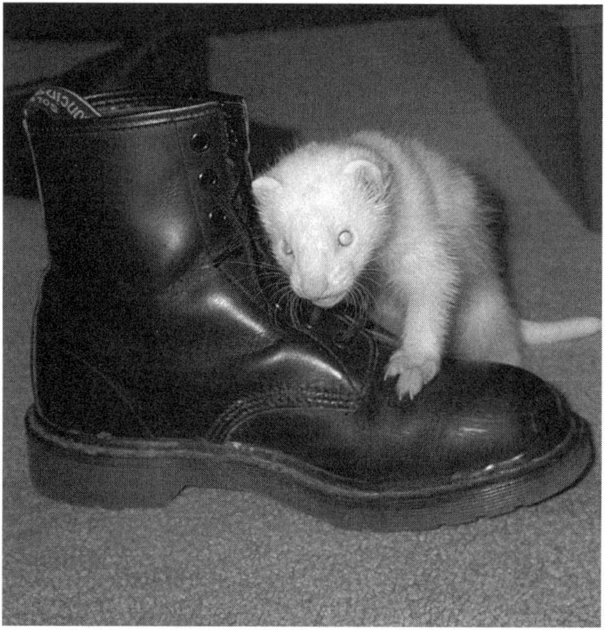

1 • Know me for a day, love me for a lifetime.

2 • Have you hugged your ferret today?

3 • Curious? Me? *Nah!*

4 • Well, it's *your* fault. I told you my litterbox should be *longer* – not wider.

5 • No! Don't look under the bed!

6 • Face it – I'm adorable.

7 • Hawkeye and Trapper used to call Frank Burns "ferret-face" on M*A*S*H. How insulting. To *us*, I mean.

8 • I do *not* look like a Slinky.

9 • I *meant* to knock over that lamp. Nice job, huh?

10 • You got me a pony!! Huh? What's a "dog?"

11 • But I can still ride it, right?

12 • No – when my tail gets all bushy like that, you may *not* use it to clean out the water bottle.

13 • I *am* behaving.

14 • Ferrets: We're not just a pet, we're an adventure!

15 • I thought the carpet *was* the toilet paper.

16 • I did *not* hide your wallet under the couch! I hid it behind the bookcase.

17 • Are you making out the shopping list? Can we get a cereal that *I* like this time?

18 • Longfellow had a pet ferret who inspired some rather lengthy poetry. Oddly enough, the ferret's name was also Longfellow.

19 • Yeah? Well, maybe *you* smell "stronger" when *you're* asleep, too, but *I'm* just not rude enough to mention it!

20 • *What* sock?

21 • I forgot where I was going.

22 • Ferret Math: When you absolutely, positively have to get another ferret.

23 • Yes, I *am* fascinating, aren't I?

24 • Who are you calling "a little squirrelly?"

25 • Born to steal.

26 • Ferrets: You can't love just one!

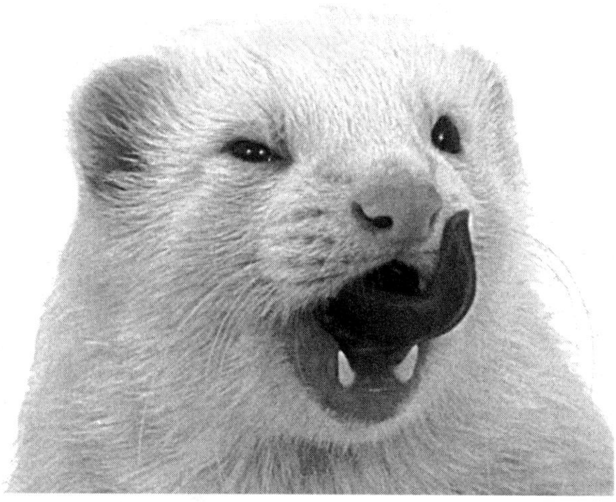

27 • You know, maybe the bag boy just forgot to put the salami in the bag! Did you ever think of that?

28 • Okay, you can dress me up – as long as our outfits don't clash!

29 • Ferrets: We give new meaning to the term "warm fuzzies."

30 • Don't you think my litterbox would look better over there?

31 • Cat toys? I think not.

32 • Isn't it enough that I had to have a bath – do you have to laugh like that?

33 • Your ferret loves you because you love him. And because you have food.

34 • I'm not being rude. I can't help that I chew with my mouth open.

35 • What? Someone spilled your soda? How strange…

36 • Ferrets make better pets than dogs. For instance, you don't have to take us for walks – any corner of the house is good enough for us!

37 • When in doubt, ask your ferret.

38 • You don't have to "ferret-proof" your home. I'll be good. I promise. No, *really!*

39 • When I stand on your head, it means I love you.

40 • "Lazy" isn't in the ferret vocabulary.

41 • Tube racing: The sport of kings!

42 • But the new ferret *likes* it when I drag her across the floor!

43 • Just so we understand – the toilet brush is *mine*, okay?

44 • I am *not* a crook!

45 • You keep saying that I'm making you climb the wall – maybe you're making *me* climb the cage!

46 • You needed a new carpet, anyway.

47 • Never say "quit!"

48 • What? Knocking over all the plants *annoys* you? You don't say!

49 • You call them "raisins," we call them "ferret fuel."

50 • The cat started it.

51 • Ferrets tend to scamper. Actually, we don't have much choice.

52 • What do you want? My litterbox was all the way over in the *next room!*

53 • Stop doing what?

54 • A raisin saved is a raisin earned.

55 • If you won't play with me, I'll just go and amuse myself. Where are your new shoes?

56 • Who upset the trash can? I'll tell you if you give me a raisin.

57 • You know your ferret runs the house when your sock drawer has a "pet door."

58 • *What* funny smell?

59 • Behind every good man there is a good ferret. And behind every good ferret, there is, well…you know.

60 • What – is there something *wrong* with sleeping in the dog's food dish?

61 • May I have this dance?

62 • Must... contact... mother... ship...

63 • Your car keys? What do they look like?

64 • I have no idea how that hole got scratched through the bottom of the couch.

65 • Stop stepping on me!

66 • A dog can be a ferret's best friend, too!

67 • You have me – what more could you possibly want?

68 • What can I say? Cute and cuddly looks good on me!

69 • Okay. You can hold me for fifteen seconds – but that's the absolute maximum!

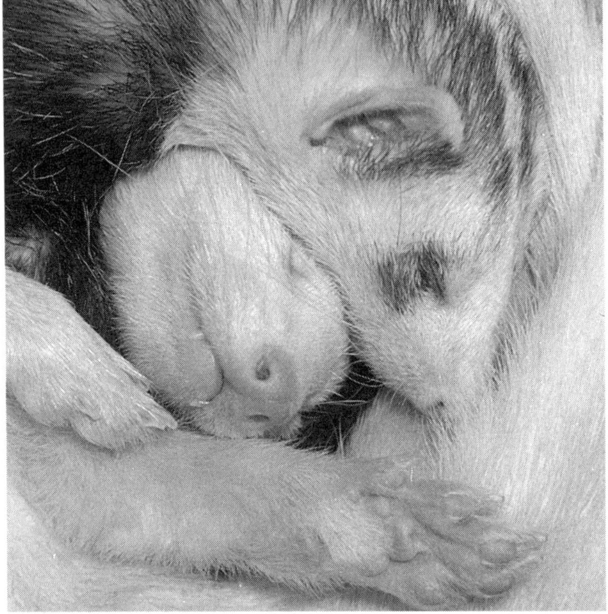

70 • A great ferret shows his greatness by the way he treats little ferrets.

71 • I'm not dead! I'm only sleeping!

72 • You haven't lived until you've taken a running start at a slippery tile floor!

73 • When you live with a ferret, chaos is normal.

74 • Nosy? Me? *Nah!*

75 • But if I *don't* exasperate you, I feel like I'm letting you down!

76 • To poop is ferret
   – to forgive divine.

77 • Nothing wrong with being a little frisky, is there?

78 • Tuck me in.

79 • Never forget that I am capable of bringing you infinite joy.

80 • What can I say – I'm flexible!

81 • I can *too* fly! Just not very far.

82 • Who are you calling a "pack rat?"

83 • A fool and his ferret are soon parted.

84 • No! Not...a ***BATH!!!***

85 • Anyone for tennis? Well, then...can I just have the ball?

86 • When you take a nap with a ferret, you'll always have sweet dreams!

87 • Wanna snuggle?

88 • Ferret owners don't need to lick their lips after a particularly good meal. We're more than happy to do that for them.

89 • *Kiss!*

90 • So I fell asleep in my litterbox – like you're perfect?

91 • Wait a minute...you think *you* own *me?* I thought it was the other way around!

92 • Of *course* I've been good. Do you think I could sleep this soundly with a guilty conscience?

93 • That's your bra? Sorry – I thought it was a hammock!

94 • Just because *you* don't sleep with your head hanging out of the bed doesn't mean it's wrong.

95 • Don't worry – I killed all the dust bunnies under your bed.

96 • Play hard.
Sleep deep.

97 • Ferrets: They're everywhere you want to be!

98 • I don't see it as the top of the bookcase so much as a goal.

99 • Ferrets aren't adorable because it makes us happy – we're adorable because it makes *you* happy!

100 • You can lead a ferret to water, but you can't make him take a bath.

101 • Well, okay... you *can* make him take a bath, but he isn't gonna like it!

102 • ***PLAY TIME!!!***

103 • Our favorite Halloween game: Bobbing for Raisins!

104 • Why do you always blame me?

105 • I don't *want* to take my medicine!

106 • I do *not* look like a fuzzy burrito.

107 • Just do it.

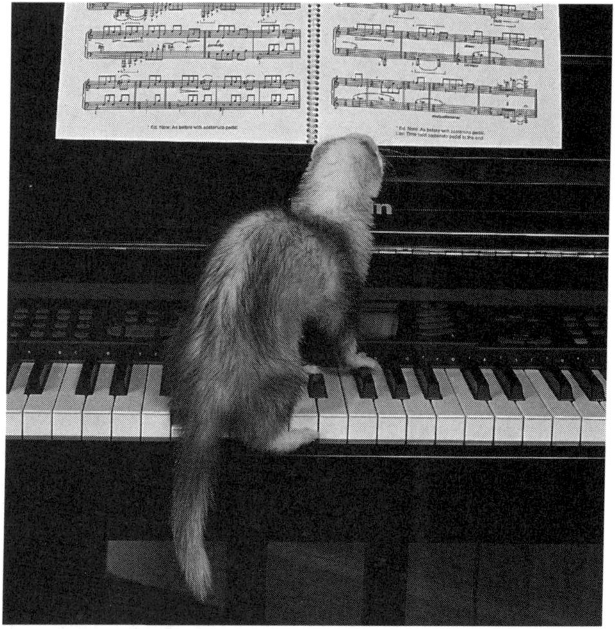

108 • Ask not what your ferret can do for you, but what you can do for your ferret!

109 • What? There's laundry missing? How strange…

110 • Yea! It's Christmas! Are all those presents for *me*?

111 • I left *your* present in the corner, by the way.

112 • I could tell you how I got up here, but then I'd have to kill you.

113 • Sorry…was this *your* shoe?

114 • That's a mail slot? I thought it was a pet door!

115 • You say, "forbidden" – I think, "challenge!"

116 • I dance, therefore I am.

117 • We're *out of raisins?* Call 911!

118 • Yes, I guess it's *possible* that Bonnie and Clyde were ferrets… what's your point?

119 • Those could be *anybody's* pawprints in the butter.

120 • I don't have big teeth, I just have small lips.

121 • Get out of where?

122 • I do that just to see you dance on one foot, you know.

123 • Ferrets make better pets than cats. For instance, we actually *listen* when you tell us not to do something. We don't technically stop *doing* it, but hey – we're listening!

124 • There's no such thing as a "bad ferret." Hey! Why are you laughing?

125 • You don't *want* another ferret. You *need* another ferret.

126 • Of course I'm trying to climb your legs. What did you expect – you weren't paying attention to me!

127 • Remember: I am capable of looking completely innocent, even when caught in the act!

128 • Trouble? Me? *Nah!*

129 • Well, you keep sticking *your* nose in *my* ears!

130 • You *sure* I can't have some of your food? I can crank up the cute, if necessary…

131 • Never pass up a chance to play!

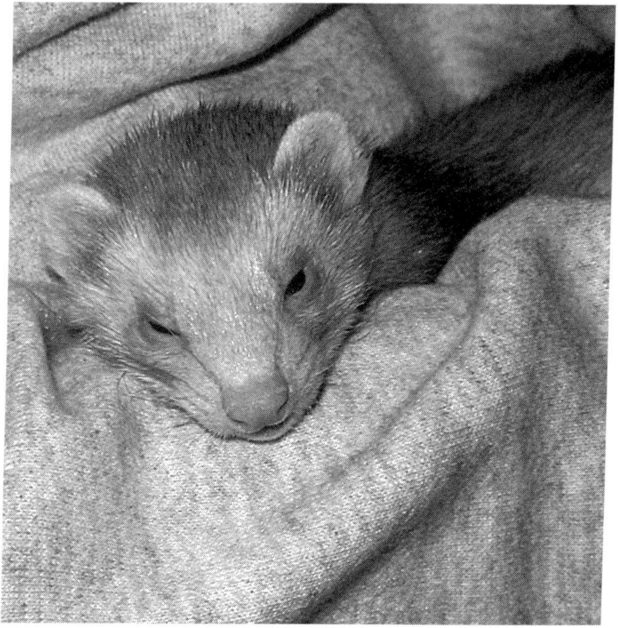

132 • Yes, I stole your heart… and I'm not giving it back.

133 • Actually, I think I'd rather have the litterbox over here.

134 • Are you *sure* it isn't time to play?

135 • Don't leave ferrets out in the sun. Not only do we get too hot, but we never seem to tan evenly.

136 • Close only counts in horseshoes and litterbox training.

137 • *What* shoe?

138 • I am *not* a weasel! Okay, technically I am…but I don't like to talk about it.

139 • At parties, ferrets always win the limbo contests.

140 • Didn't you *want* holes in your screen door?

141 • A *bath*room? I don't like the sound of that...

142 • Elderly ferrets like to move to Florida and complain about the kits these days.

143 • You can have the new toy – I want the box!

144 • Sigh.

145 • I may be small, but I make a big impression.

146 • What? There's garbage all over the kitchen floor? How strange…

147 • Don't worry about the rug…just tell people it's part of the pattern!

148 • You call them "mishaps." We call them Ferret Follies!

149 • Let's play – I bet you'll get tired before I do!

150 • If ferrets had opposable thumbs, we'd rule the world.

151 • Ferrets rule the world anyway.

152 • I am *not* a kleptomaniac!

153 • Of *course* I love you.
That's what I *do*.

154 • It is believed that ferrets may have been responsible for the strange event later known as The Great Sock Market Crash of 1929.

155 • Ferrets *would* play football, but we can't fit the ball under the couch.

156 • The wild prairie ferret used to roam the Old West, pouncing on the feet of passing cowboys and stealing their socks.

157 • Ferrets make better buddies. Just ask any of us!

158 • You don't choose a ferret – a ferret chooses you.

159 • Ferrets don't typically "chat" online. There's no emoticon for "Give me a treat!"

160 • What's this stuff in the bottle labeled "musk?" Smells pretty good!

161 • I wasn't lost. *I* knew where I was.

162 • Love me, love my many idiosyncrasies!

163 • Define "stolen."

164 • Don't worry, I won't get stuck.

165 • Um… I'm stuck.

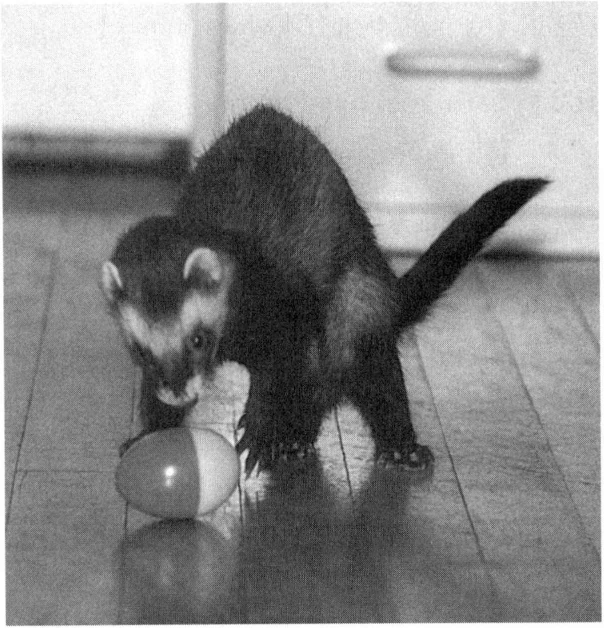

166 • Please clean the litterbox. Who knows – I might actually *use* it someday!

167 • What? You can't find the remote? How strange…

168 • Of *course* I'm using my cute and adorable qualities to get you to give me a treat. Do you expect me to let all of this go to waste?

169 • Hey, I don't know what that was doing under the couch. It was supposed to be behind the TV.

170 • Tag! You're it!

171 • No – wait! I *like* dirty ears! Really!

172 • Socks – *filled with treats?* This Christmas thing is ***GREAT!!!***

173 • Ferrets are a whole lotta love in a tiny little package.

174 • What – is the litterbox *not* a good place to dig?

175 • If you didn't want me to climb on my cage, why does it look like it's made out of all these little ladders?

176 • Occasionally, ferrets wish we had wings. Can you just imagine the mischief we could get into if we could *fly?*

177 • Ferrets often know when you're happy, and we usually know when you're sad – but we *always* know when you have treats!

178 • Some "accidents" are on purpose.

179 • Happiness is a pile of warm towels after a bath.

180 • Just think of it as fertilizer.

181 • Ferrets don't ski – but we're great sledders!

182 • The kitchen was like that when I got here.

183 • Curiosity. It isn't just for cats.

184 • Having a ferret isn't a matter of life and death…it's a lot more important than that!

185 • Come on, let me out of the cage! There's stuff that needs to be put away!

186 • If God made anything cuter than a ferret, He must have kept it for Himself.

187 • Just put a litterbox in every corner of the house. That way, *everyone's* happy!

188 • I didn't do it. *Honest!*

189 • Okay, I did it.

190 • You think I'm trouble *now*... just wait until you see me on a sugar buzz!

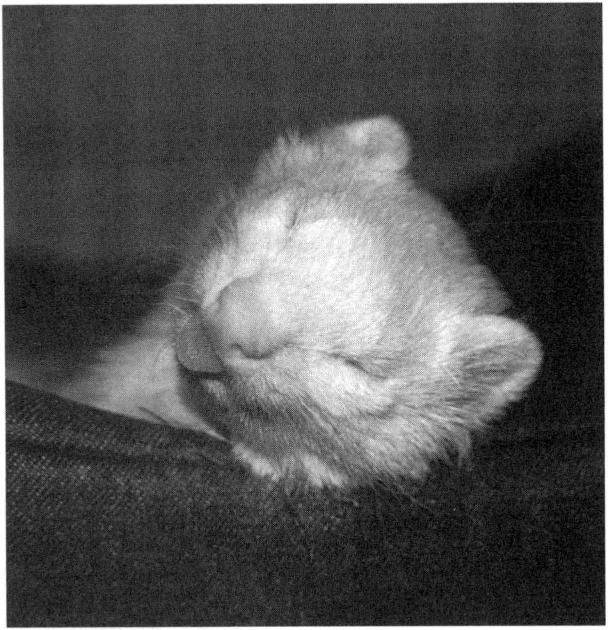

191 • Hey, that could be *anybody's* fur in the spaghetti.

- 192 • Everybody into the hammock!
- 193 • There's room for one more!
- 194 • Isn't it about time for some new toys?
- 195 • Another ferret? Why? Aren't I enough for you?
- 196 • You can never have too much fun!
- 197 • Oops. That's embarrassing.

198 • I wasn't stealing your stuffed animals – I was keeping them safe!

199 • Ferrets love attention almost as much as we love treats.

200 • *Almost.*

201 • Hey, maybe *you're* under *my* feet! Did you ever think of that?

202 • Ferrets are happy animals. Wouldn't *you* be, if you were a ferret?

203 • Well, that plant needed to be re-potted, anyway.

204 • Yeah, well, you look pretty goofy yourself, sometimes!

205 • A true friend doesn't look at a ferret with his eyes, but with his heart.

206 • So many socks – so little time!

207 • You want to trim my nails? But I *just* got them the right length!

208 • Happiness, ferret be thy name.

209 • Mischievous? Me? *Nah!*

210 • Of *course* there are ferrets in Heaven. How else could you call it Heaven?

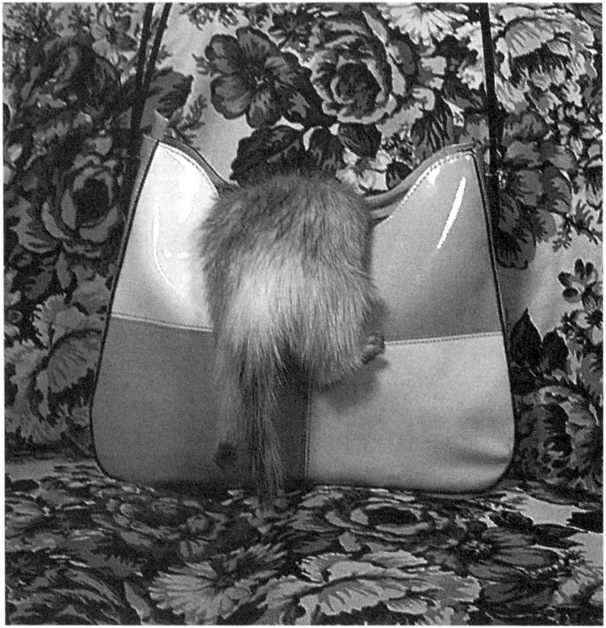

211 • But *everything's* my business.

212 • Go for it!

213 • Are those groceries for me?

214 • Hey! Watch where you're walking!

215 • Whoever said that money can't buy happiness must have never heard of ferrets.

216 • There really is no such thing as "ferret-proof."

217 • When in doubt, improvise.

218 • Blame it on the cat!

219 • Sorry…was I sleeping too soundly again?

220 • When you've had a bad day, give your ferret a hug. There's no better cure for the blues than fuzz therapy!

221 • Are you sure Rikki-Tikki-Tavi wasn't a ferret?

222 • The Few, the Proud…the Ferrets!

223 • Most of a ferret's time is spent wrestling with his inner kit.

224 • I'm not in your way at all, am I?

225 • Ferrets don't go to therapists, though we probably should.

226 • The plant started it.

227 • Ferrets need a safe place all to themselves, where they feel they can do anything they please. Your home will do just fine.

228 • I just want to see what's under your foot.

229 • There's no better feeling than being tucked in.

230 • Every day is a new chance for mischief.

231 • Do you mind? I'm *busy*, here!

232 • I wonder what will happen if I put my cold, wet nose right *here*.

233 • Did you not like that?

234 • Everybody do the conga!

235 • We're ferrets. We try harder.

236 • Pay attention to me!

237 • Everyone on the sleeping pile!

238 • I know I'm not allowed *on* the couch. I was *in* the couch.

239 • Time for the Weasel War Dance!

240 • When a ferret is your friend, *every* day is Thanksgiving.

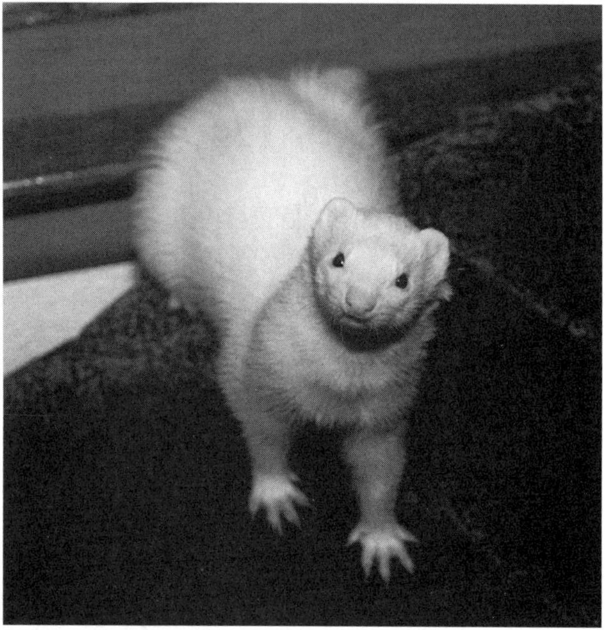

241 • Well, sometimes I wish *you* were better trained, too!

242 • Ferrets are very honest creatures. Think about it – has your ferret ever lied to you?

243 • That you know of?

244 • Ferrets make strange – but warm and cuddly – bedfellows!

245 • The longer you hold a ferret, the better life becomes.

246 • To ferret or not to ferret, that is the question.

247 • *Another* bath? Will I *ever* be clean enough for you?

248 • Someone once attempted to train Seeing-Eye Ferrets, but they just kept walking their owners into walls and giggling.

249 • Bandit? You're naming me *Bandit*? How original!

250 • An itch in time saves nine!

251 • Cat owners hate to clean the litterbox. Ferret owners love this simple chore…they're just so darn glad their ferret decided to *use* it for a change!

252 • I don't bite, but watch out for my human!

253 • Look – *you* bought the powdered sugar…what did you expect?

254 • I have no idea what happened to your briefcase.

255 • Never look a gift ferret in the mouth. Trust me.

256 • Senseless: A word that can be used to describe the actions of a ferret to a human being.

257 • Ferrets are the center of the universe.

258 • Ferrets would love to be firehouse mascots. Sliding down that pole looks like fun!

259 • Oh no! You waxed the floor!

260 • Your ferret fully appreciates you. Do you fully appreciate your ferret?

261 • Ferrets can read maps. We just can't fold them.

262 • Okay. This was a mistake. You wanna get me out of here now?

263 • Ferrets are not vegetarians. Remember that!

264 • Make it up as you go along!

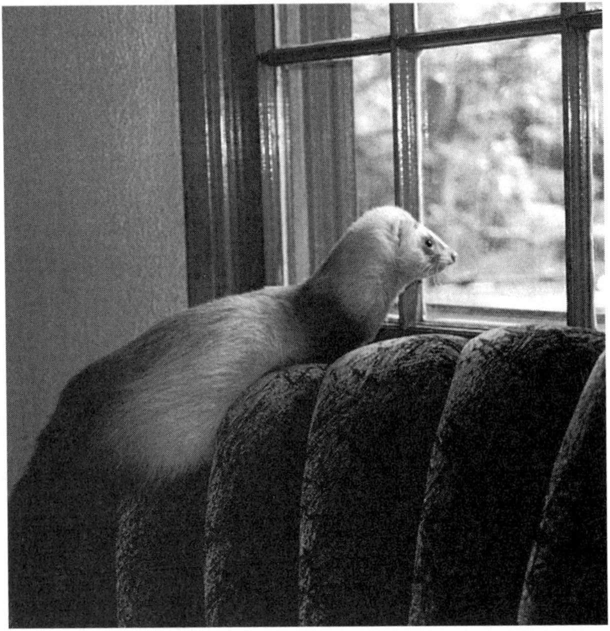

265 • Some call me the Carpet Shark.

266 • I did it my way!

267 • Senseless: A word that can be used to describe the actions of a human being to a ferret.

268 • I dance, therefore I am... a ferret!

269 • Don't mind the racket – we're just playing.

270 • Okay, easy now...just drop the sock and no one gets hurt!

271 • A rolling ferret gathers no moss.

272 • I'm not fat, I'm big-furred.

273 • The vet wants to take my temperature? Are you going to permit this barbarism?

274 • Ferrets don't need plastic surgery. You can't improve on perfection!

275 • Never use your ferret as a lawn jockey.

276 • Ah... to be a kit again...

277 • I was born to play.

278 • Ferrets have poor credit ratings.

279 • I only sneeze on people I like... and I like you!

280 • Mind if I walk right under you until you trip?

281 • You know that antique vase in the foyer? You didn't really *like* it, did you?

282 • There's the phone. I'll get it.

283 • I'm not *always* mischievous. Sometimes I'm asleep.

284 • Are you *sure* you weren't getting me a treat?

285 • Ferrets don't have any bad habits.

286 • Oh, the little ferret? I dragged her behind the couch.

287 • Ferrets don't golf. It's the pants.

288 • Older ferrets still remember with sadness the Great Raisin Famine of '89.

289 • Mind if I put my tail in your soup?

290 • I do *not* look like a furry dachshund.

291 • Please don't call me a "speed bump." I'm just resting.

292 • Itch break!

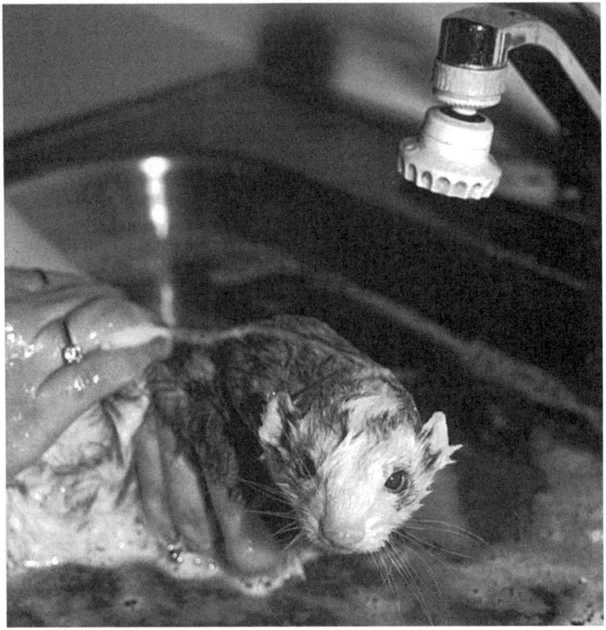

293 • How do you *know* there aren't any sharks in my bath water?

294 • Oh look! I'm under the rug!

295 • Ferrets are all insane. But we know this, and we're comfortable with it.

296 • You *won't* grant my every wish? Why not?

297 • Your feet smell *divine*!

298 • I'm not a rodent!

299 • Define "missing."

300 • Ferrets aren't allowed in fancy restaurants, because we always slurp our soup.

301 • I'm sorry. Did I shed all over your new sweater?

302 • We're not fighting – this is how we play.

303 • What do you mean, you just gave me a treat? I have no recollection of that!

304 • Elderly ferrets are very self-conscious about their gray fur.

305 • Do I *have* to get out of the refrigerator?

306 • The Great Pyramids of Egypt were actually built by alien ferrets from Atlantis.

307 • Oh, those are your bell-bottoms? I thought it was one of my tunnel toys.

308 • What are you hiding behind that door?

309 • The world is my litterbox!

310 • Ferrets would have never invented "de-caf."

311 • Charlie Chaplin had a ferret. It was black and white and refused to utter a sound until the early thirties.

312 • Ferrets can't balance a checkbook.

313 • Curl up with a good ferret.

314 • *Time to eat a crunchy!*

315 • Your glasses? What did they look like?

316 • Oh, I'm sorry – is that *my* paw in your pasta salad?

317 • Kiss me, you fool!

318 • Some people find musk very alluring...

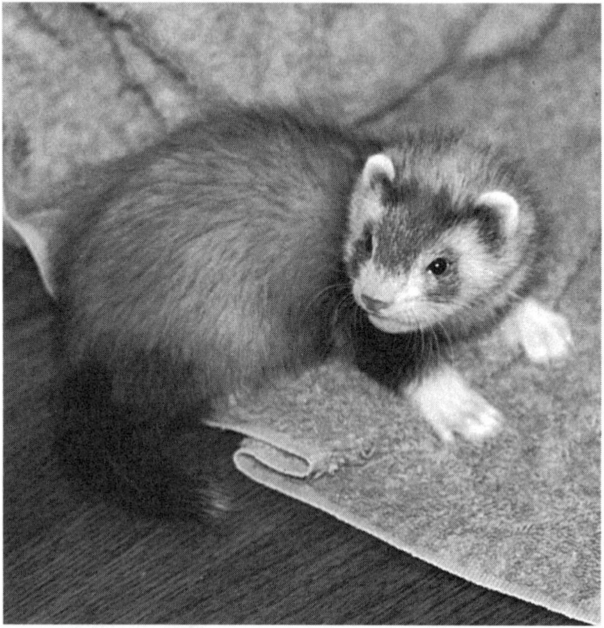

319 • No, I *couldn't* possibly be any cuter.

320 • Well, I came *close* to the litterbox – doesn't that count for something?

321 • I fear nothing. Mostly.

322 • Ferrets do not depreciate.

323 • You think I dance funny? At least I don't do the macarena!

324 • Never feed your ferret from the table. Just put your plate on the floor where he can reach it.

325 • Ferrets don't believe in gravity.

326 • Who *does?*

327 • I'll stop bugging you to let me out of my cage if you let me out of my cage!

328 • You can never play with your ferret too much.

329 • Ferrets can't program VCRs, but we're still willing to get in there and give it a try!

330 • Ferrets operate on the principle of entropy.

331 • Do I *have* to get out of the TV cart?

332 • Stop rubbing your feet on the carpet before you pick me up!

333 • Were you reading that magazine?

334 • I *know* you can't reach me here! That's why I'm sleeping here.

335 • Our favorite musical: *My Ferret Lady.*

336 • Kits will be kits!

337 • Why do I have to stay in my cage when guests visit? Why not let *me* out and put *them* in the cage?

338 • Take time to stop and smell the ferrets!

339 • It's ten o'clock – do you know where your socks are?

340 • Yawn!

341 • Wanna see my Dance of Joy?

342 • *What* incessant scratching sound?

343 • I'm *not* throwing a tantrum!
I'm not I'm not I'm not I'm *not!*

344 • Policemen are really ferrets in disguise. Why else would anyone call them "The Fuzz?"

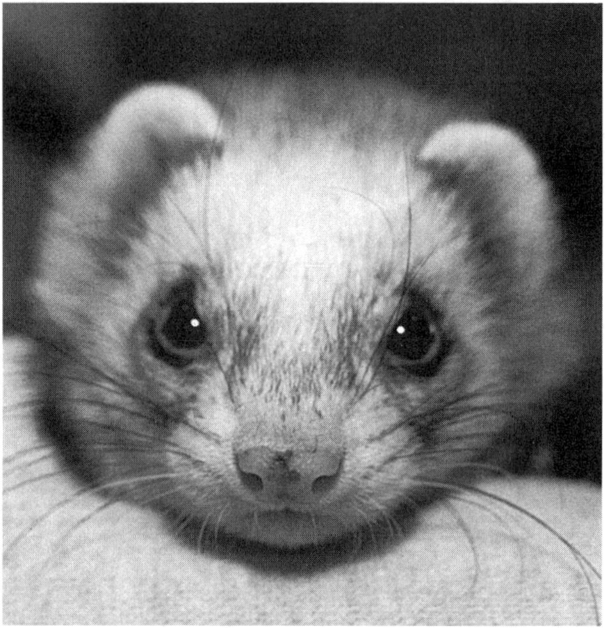

345 • I love the smell of unwashed feet in the morning.

346 • For a ferret, *every* day is time for Trick or Treats!

347 • Why, yes, I *am* precious! Thank you for noticing!

348 • S-T-R-E-T-C-H

349 • We do our own stunts!

350 • I have no idea how this electrical cord got in my mouth.

351 • Yes, I'm inside the couch. So?

352 • A paper bag? For *me?* Oh, you *shouldn't have!*

353 • It *is* a very nice bowl. But I like to eat my kibble off the floor.

354 • I may not be a genius, but I can still figure out where you keep the raisins!

355 • What's my favorite toy to play with? You!

356 • Hey! Watch where you're sitting!

357 • Mind if I climb up your leg?

358 • Ferret Math: Just keep adding more ferrets!

359 • I told you I could get up here.

360 • There's no such thing as a boring ferret.

361 • Don't just stand there – help me down!

362 • It's *tunnelin' time!*

363 • If this is a "manicure," where's the nail polish?

364 • The litterbox was like that when I got here.

365 • Albino ferrets look like fuzzy little angels.

366 • No! Not a *futon!* How am I going to get into *that?*

367 • A pest? Me? *Nah!*

368 • Just call me Wile E. Ferret, Super Genius!

369 • Well, *I* think it fits.

370 • Fresh, minty breath? P-U!

371 • Stash some food away for a rainy day.

372 • You want to cover the bottom of my cage? How about covering it in raisins?

373 • You call it trouble, we call it destiny.

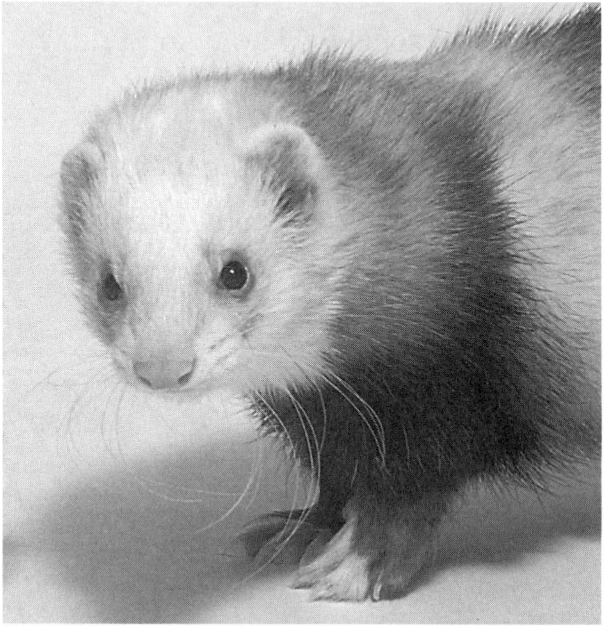

374 • No!
Don't look under the sofa!

375 • I don't care *what* you say – I *can* dig all the way to China!

376 • Don't call me Rat Tail – I'm very sensitive, thank you!

377 • Let's go to the park again! Can *I* play on the slide this time?

378 • Oh no…not ear cleaning time again!

379 • Mind if I walk all over you?

380 • Maybe *you're* the one that needs a bath!

381 • A smelly t-shirt? Cool!

382 • That tickles!

383 • You're washing my *hammock*? But I finally got the smell just right!

384 • A leash? That goes on you, right?

385 • Are you sure it isn't a ferret store? The sign says "curiosity shop!"

386 • Who are you calling a mustelid? Oh. Right.

387 • Can you believe ferrets used to have to *work* for their keep?

388 • The dog is wet – and you think *I* smell?

389 • What can I say – sock-collecting is my hobby!

390 • Ferrets aren't pets – we're a way of life!

391 • I don't need a pedigree – I've got *ferretude!*

392 • Care to tango?

393 • If a ferret licks your nose, it's good luck.

394 • Don't judge a ferret 'til you've walked a mile on his paws.

395 • A necktie? I though it was a dangly toy!

396 • Does my water *have* to stay in the dish?

397 • Tough! *Splashsplashsplashsplash!*

398 • Hey! You woke me up! Stop that!

399 • *Crunch, crunch!*

400 • Of course I'm hoarding pens – I may want to write a novel someday!

401 • Or at least a tell-all exposé about you taking away all of my pens…

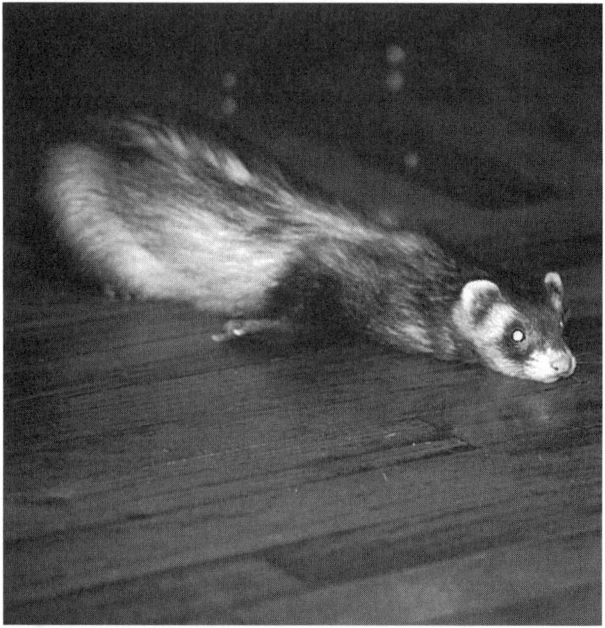

402 • What are you yelling at *me* for? I didn't tell you to step in it!

403 • The dog and I have a deal – I get the socks, he gets the shoes!

404 • Do I *have to* get out of your guest's purse?

405 • Wheee!

406 • Of *course* I'm having fun! It's what I do!

407 • By the pricking of my thumbs, something ferrety this way comes.

408 • What? All the books fell off the shelf? How strange…

409 • I poop, therefore I am!

410 • I just love that crashing sound! Mind if I break something else?

411 • I can't really *help* being this cute!

412 • Ferrets: Fur-covered love!

413 • My front feet were in the litterbox – doesn't that count for something?

414 • I ate a bug!

415 • Why not make a game of looking for your socks? That way, it's fun for both of us!

416 • Pick me up!

417 • Put me down!

418 • I *have* to explore the garbage can – it's uncharted territory!

419 • Hey! Leggo of my scruff!

420 • I didn't break your vase – gravity did!

421 • Yeesh… don't you have a sense of humor?

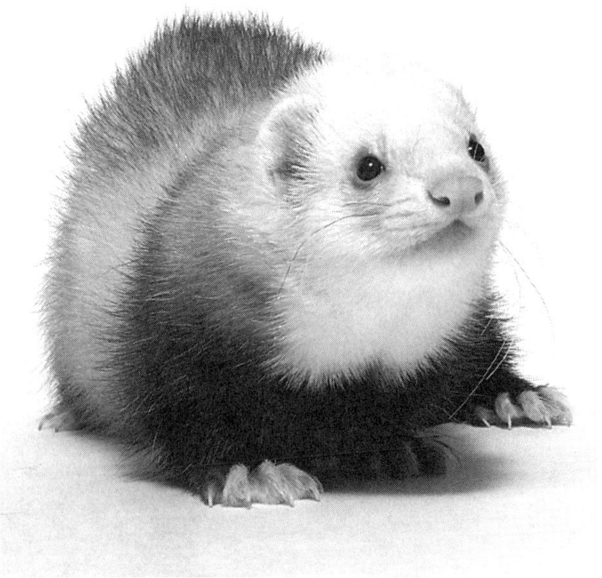

422 • The *other* glove? I don't know what you're talking about.

423 • Don't let anyone tell you that I'm not domesticated!

424 • Dooka, dooka!

425 • I do *not* look like an otter when I swim!

426 • Okay, I do… but I'm much trimmer!

427 • I really hate the vacuum cleaner, you know.

428 • Yes, I know there's food stashed all over the house. What's your point?

429 • You think I dance funny? You should see the way I sleep!

430 • No. You can't nickname me "Thud."

431 • You have *no idea* how much mischief I can get into when I really apply myself!

432 • I'm not only good
 – I'm good *for* you!

433 • I'm not looking for stuff to steal – I'm shopping!

434 • I'm way too charming for your own good!

435 • You know…you have a tendency to nag. You may want to work on that.

436 • Didn't you *want* holes in your carpet?

437 • I may be little, but I've got a big heart!

438 • Freud's ferret had the strangest dreams…

439 • Of *course* I'm fun. What did you expect?

440 • I love my hammock!

441 • Bewitched, bothered, and bewildered accurately describes most ferret owners.

442 • Like piling your guests' coats on the bed wasn't asking for trouble.

443 • I don't want a bath – but I wouldn't mind eating the soap!

444 • *Chuckle!*

445 • Leather gloves? Yup – they're filed behind that chair.

446 • I know there's a prize down here in my food dish some- where…

447 • Now, *this* is a hissy fit!

448 • Hey – at least I smell better than the cat box!

449 • *What* mail?

450 • Do I *have* to get out of the box spring?

451 • A water bottle? How am I supposed to splash around in *that?*

452 • I have albino jeans? *Cool!*

453 • Neat! You got a leather couch! Where am I going to hide that?

454 • Why should I do a trick? I know you'll give me the treat anyway.

455 • Sometimes you just have to lie down and plan your next move.

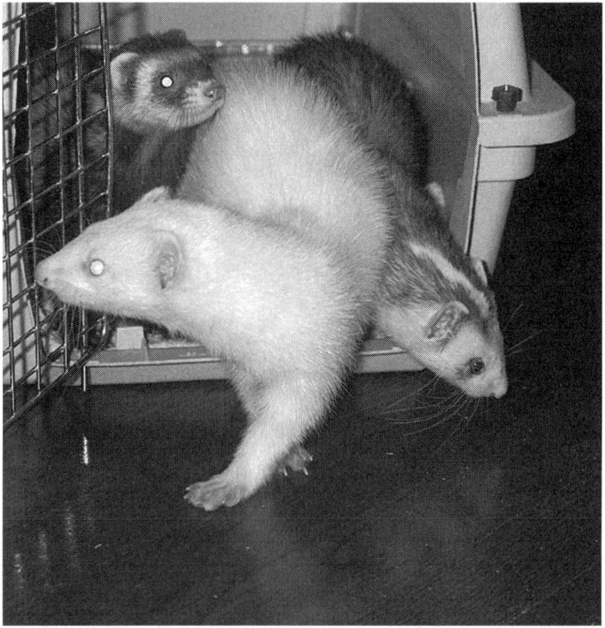

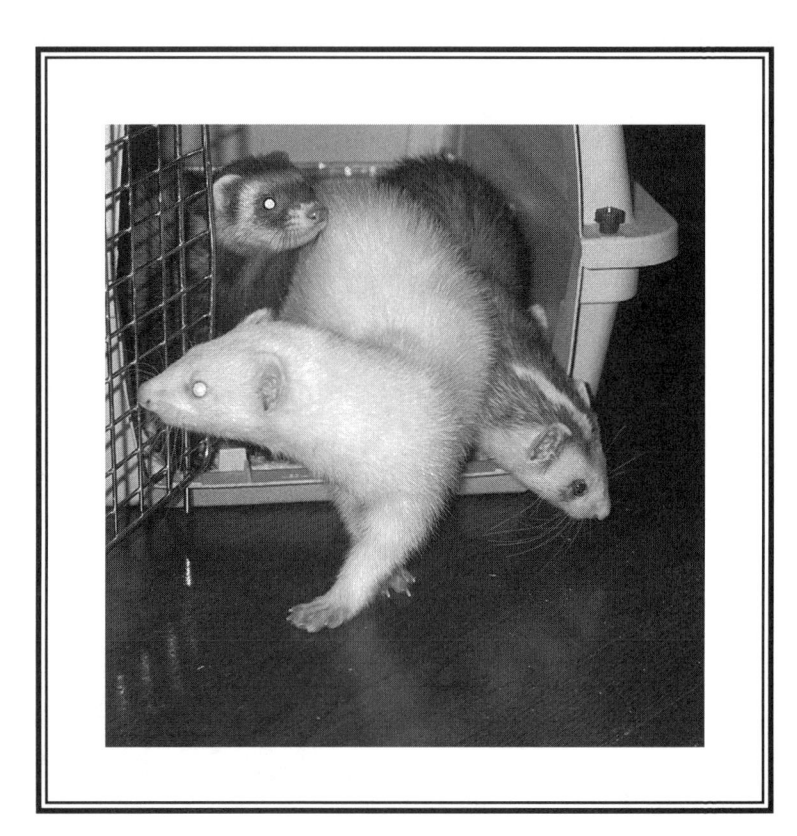

456 • What's that interesting smell?

457 • Hey! Someone broke into my hidey-hole and stole all my stuff! Call the cops!

458 • Face it – one look at these eyes, and there's no *way* you can punish me!

459 • Ferret Math: Resistance is futile!

460 • Don't you wish *you* were a ferret, too?

461 • Put down that shampoo bottle before somebody gets hurt!

462 • I *am* being careful.

463 • You're not supposed to use a cotton swab to clean my ears – you're supposed to use your tongue!

464 • I was just checking how many tissues come in a box.

465 • There were exactly one hundred thirty-two tissues in the box. Thought you'd like to know.

466 • Umm… you're out of tissues.

467 • If I stare at you long enough, I bet I can hypnotize you into giving me treats!

468 • I just *know* there's buried treasure in *one* of these plants!

469 • Yeah? Well, maybe *you* look absurd after a bath, too!

470 • I'm living as large as I can!

471 • Play with me some more!

472 • Actually, you've told me not to climb the cage one hundred and *twelve* times.

473 • Yeah, I'm flat…so?

474 • I'm bananas for bananas!

475 • Never pass up a chance to snooze!

476 • I didn't see any straw in your soda…

477 • Our favorite comedy: *Ferret Bueller's Day Off!*

478 • You *know* I can melt your heart!

479 • Darling? Me? *Absolutely!*

480 • I'm going to go to sleep in your hand. Don't move it for a few hours, okay?

481 • Of *course* I'm smiling! You're rubbing my ears, aren't you?

482 • But I thought you *enjoyed* using the broom!

483 • Do you mind? I'm having a battle to the death with my shadow here!

484 • What can I say? I'm determined!

485 • He that lieth down with dogs, shall rise up with fleas.

486 • Ferrets are like potato chips…

487 • Of course I use my litterbox –
I slept in it just last night!

488 • You can never have too many treats!

489 • Beware of albinos bearing gifts.

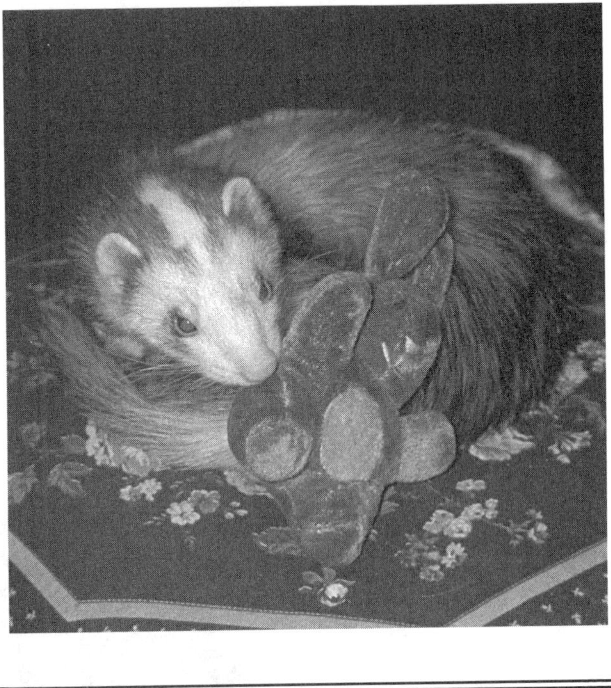

490 • That's a stuffed animal? Oh, how embarrassing… I thought it was my date!

491 • You never know – there might be a market for Ferret-Poop-in-a-Jar!

492 • Ferrets are a *natural* stimulant.

493 • I wasn't stealing the remote! I just wanted to watch *Leave it to Beaver!*

494 • Missing socks? We ferrets have a pact with the laundry gods.

495 • Everyone is my friend.

496 • My tail smells grape!

497 • My whiskers tickle? You don't say.

498 • I wasn't looking where I was going.

499 • ***NAP TIME!!!***

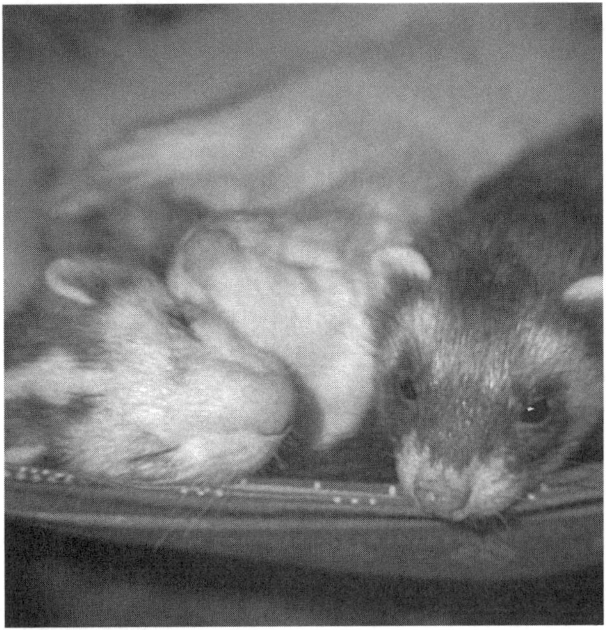

500 • Ferrets leave tiny little pawprints on your heart.

Modern Ferret Magazine

Since 1994, Mary and Eric Shefferman have worked to create a ferret resource that they and their ferrets could be proud of. The result is *Modern Ferret* Magazine — chosen as one of the 50 Most Notable Magazine Launches of 1995 and one of the 12 Best Magazines in the Magazine Industry in 1999.

When you read *Modern Ferret*...

* Your ferrets will be better trained
* Your ferrets will live in a less stressful environment
* You'll recognize the signs of illness sooner and be better equipped to address them
* Your home will be safer for your ferrets
* You'll learn from the experiences of your fellow ferret owners around the world
* You'll be aware of the latest ferret medical developments and treatments
* You'll understand your ferrets' behaviors
* You'll be prepared with the solutions to your ferret problems
* You'll have more fun with your ferrets — and your ferrets will have more fun with you!

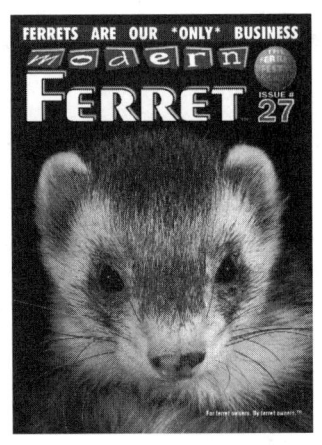

For a subscription to *Modern Ferret* send $27.95 payable to:

Modern Ferret
PO Box 1007
Smithtown NY 11787

see our web site for more information
www.modernferret.com

Books by *Modern Ferret:*

500 Things My Ferret Told Me: $14.95
You'll laugh. You'll learn. You'll love your ferret!
A fun gift book filled with the things you *know* your ferret is thinking.

The Wit and Wisdom of the Modern Ferrets: $12.95
A Ferret's Perspective on Ferret Care
Ferret care tips columns from *Modern Ferret* magazine written from a ferret's point of view.

Shipping:
Please include $4.95 shipping for the first book and $1.00 shipping for each additional book.

Sales Tax:
New York State residents please add applicable sales tax.

To order, send check or money order payable to:
Ferret Trading Post
PO Box 1007
Smithtown NY 11787

for faster service and to see the newest books, order online at:
http://www.FerretTradingPost.com

THE MODERN Ferret News

The *Modern Ferret News* is a **FREE** pet ferret care information e-newsletter that comes right in your e-mail! *Sign up today!*

- Timely pet ferret care tips
- Announcements and news
- Advance notice of new product releases
- Health tips
- Schedule dates
- Sales and special offers at ferret web sites
- Updates on Mary & Eric Shefferman and their ferrets

http://www.FerretNews.com

While you're there, be sure to check out the article archives!

Everything You Want!

T-Shirts • Mugs • Mousepads • Tote Bags

New designs all the time!

Are you the #1 Ferret Mom?

ORDER ONLINE TODAY!

www.FerretDesigns.com

501 • Ferrets *can't* count.